Contents

Tannery Drift School
Tannery Drift
Royston
Herts
SG8 5DE

Introduction

Queen Elizabeth I

A monarchy is a type of government that has a single ruler, the monarch. In the UK, the **monarch** is called the king or queen.

The role of monarch lasts for life, and is **hereditary**. This means that the role of monarch stays in one family. When a monarch dies, the oldest son or the oldest daughter (if there isn't a son) inherits the throne.

Queen Elizabeth II belongs to a family that has ruled for hundreds of years.

Queen Victoria
(1837–1901)
+
Prince Albert

King Edward VII
(1901–1910)
+
Queen Alexandra

The Princess
Alice

King George V
(1910–1936)
+
Queen Mary

King George VI
(1936–1952)
+
Queen Elizabeth (The Queen Mother)

Queen Elizabeth II
(1952–Present)
+
Prince Philip

The Royal Family Tree.

These flags show some of the countries ruled by our monarch.

Long ago, most of the countries in Europe were monarchies. People believed that kings and queens were chosen by God to rule over them. But these days most people don't believe that. Some European countries, such as France, have abolished the monarchy and become a **republic** instead.

Jacques Chirac is the President of France

This map of Europe shows which countries are still monarchies

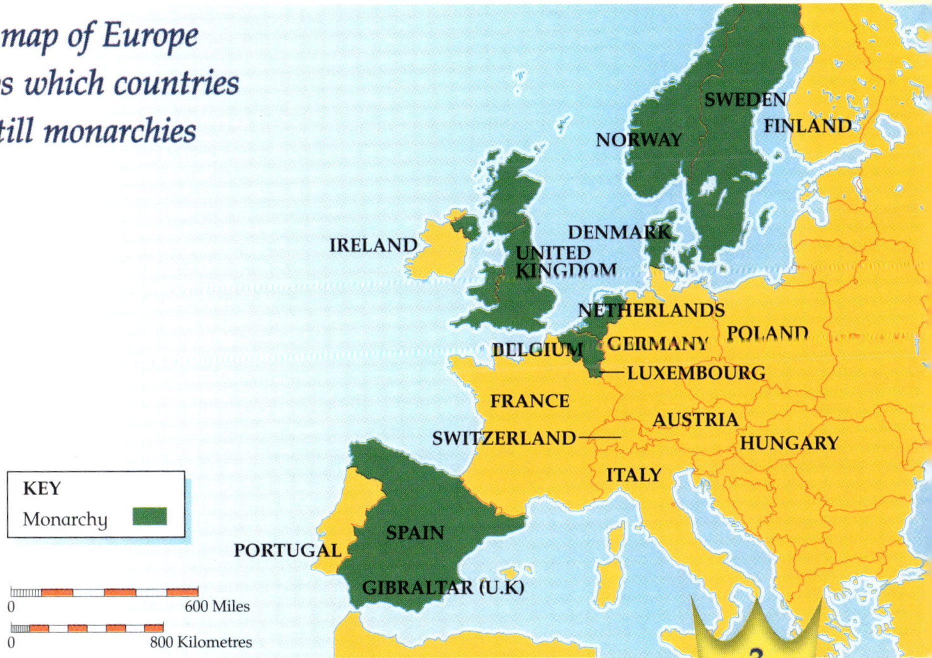

Other countries, such as the UK, Norway, Sweden, Denmark, the Netherlands and Spain, have kept the monarchy, but taken away most of its political power. In these monarchies, the people choose the **government**, and the government rules on behalf of the monarch.

The Swedish royal family

So do we still need a monarchy in the UK?

In the debate about the future of the monarchy in the UK we look at three choices:

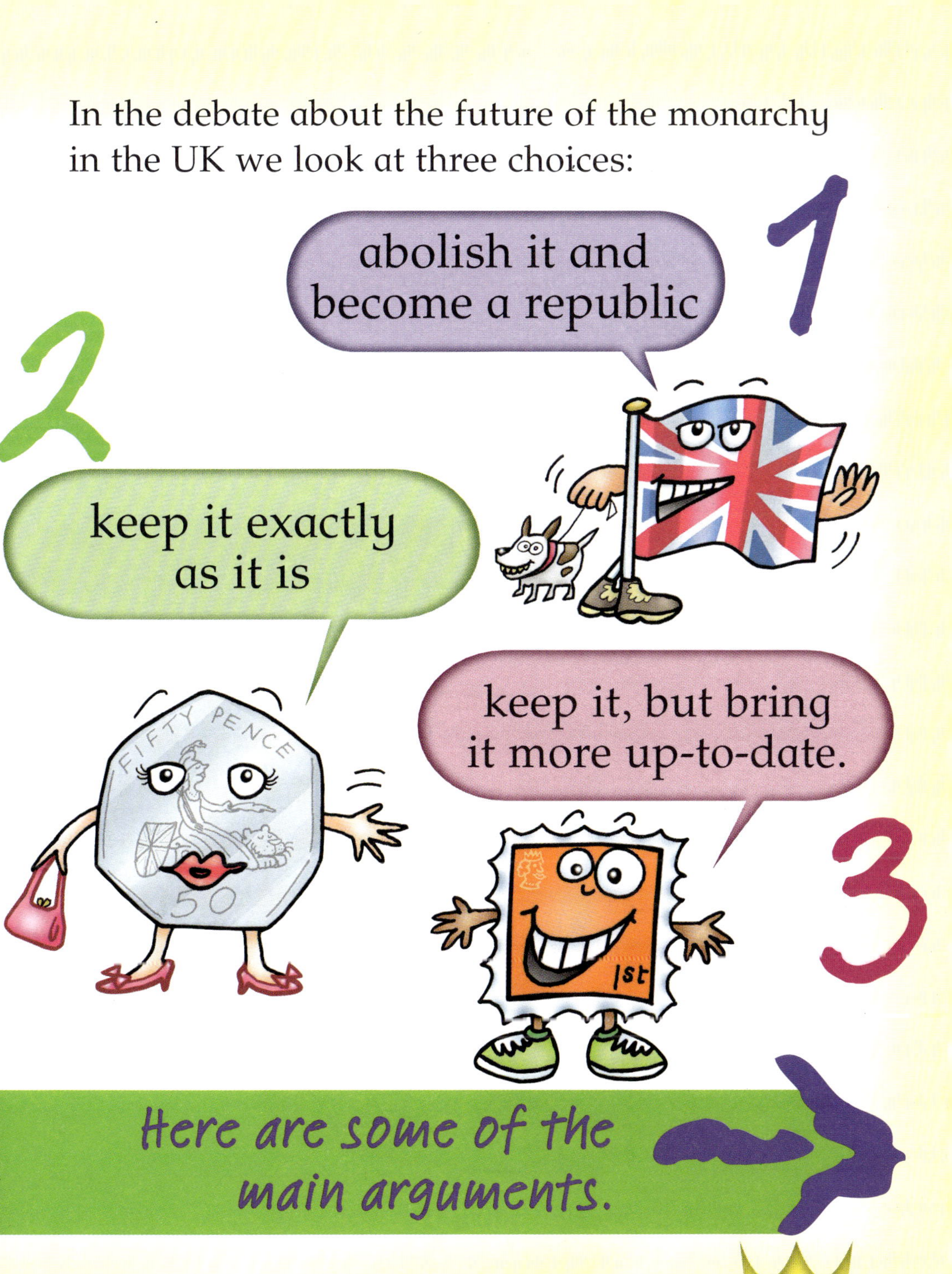

Why we should abolish the monarchy

1 The monarchy no longer plays a useful part in government.

In the UK, the monarch does not play an active part in politics.

The government decides how to run the country and the monarch's job is simply to give his or her approval.

The Prime Minister at work with other members of the government.

The monarch's approval is called the Royal Assent. The Royal Assent gives the government the legal power to carry out its ideas.

However, as the Royal Assent is now always given, the Queen does not really have any power over the government. Although it is her job to appoint a new **prime minister**, she actually always chooses the person government has voted for.

The Queen giving the Royal Assent.

Did you know?

Royal Assent was last given in person by the monarch in 1854. The Royal Assent has not been refused in nearly 200 years.

2 The monarchy costs too much.

The Queen is one of the wealthiest people in the world, and yet the British people still make payments to her from their **taxes** each year.

There are two main types of payment to the royal family:

- The Civil List. This is a yearly **grant** paid to three members of the royal family: the Queen, the Queen Mother and the Duke of Edinburgh. It comes to millions of pounds a year.

- The grants-in-aid. These grants pay for the Queen's houses and transport. They also come to millions of pounds each year.

3 The monarchy is out of date.

A monarchy is based on the idea that some people are born to rule over others. It singles out one family for a life of wealth and privilege.

The majority of people now believe in equal rights for men and women, but in most monarchies the sons of kings and queens are more important than the daughters. Queen Elizabeth II has four children – Charles, Anne, Andrew and Edward. But although Anne, the Princess Royal, is the second oldest, all her brothers and their children come before her in line to the throne.

This is the **order of succession** in the UK.

Charles, Prince of Wales

Andrew, Duke of York (the elder of Charles' two younger brothers)

Prince William (Charles' elder son)

Prince Henry (Charles' younger son)

Beatrice of York (Andrew's elder child – he has no sons)

Modern Britain is a **multicultural society**, which includes people of different religions and beliefs. The British monarch is head of the **Church of England**, which, until 50 years ago, represented the spiritual beliefs of most of the nation.

The Queen and the Archbishop of Canterbury, who is the most senior bishop in England.

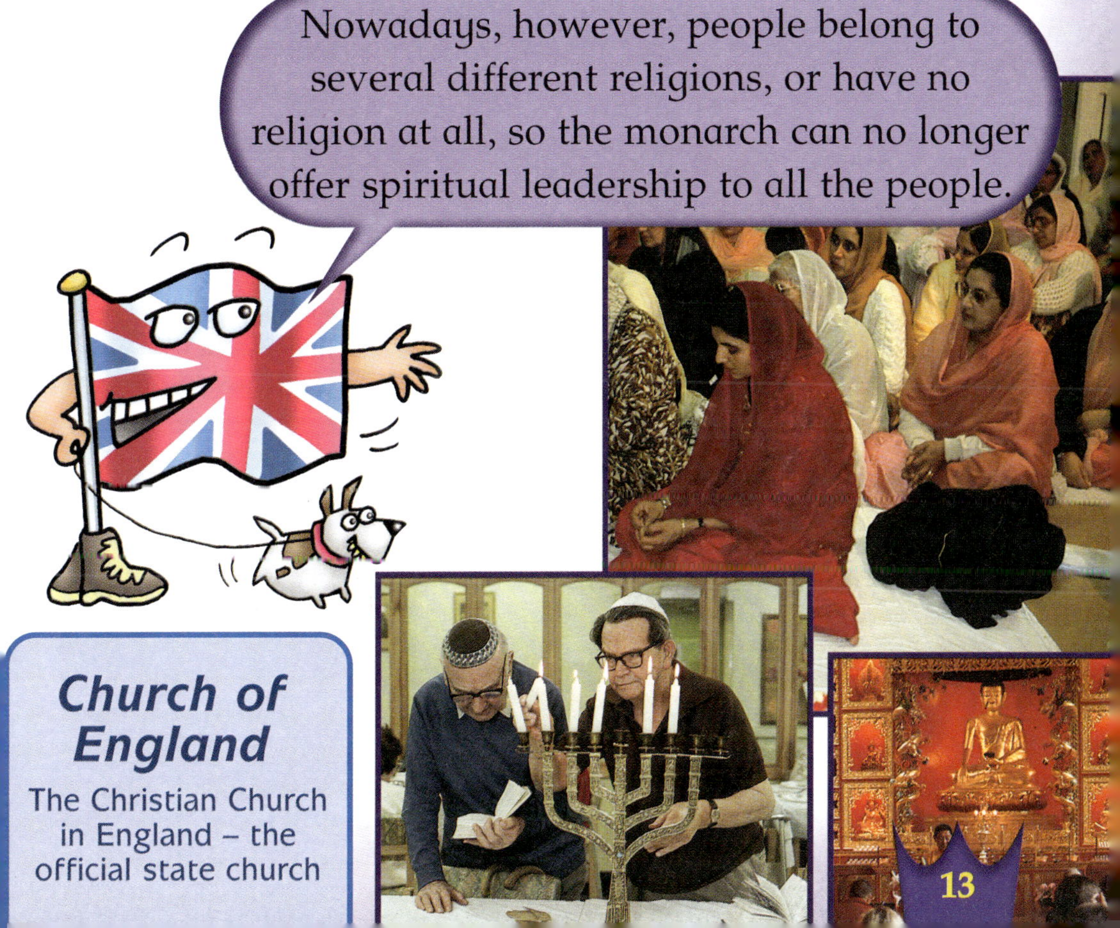

Church of England

The Christian Church in England – the official state church

Why we should keep the monarchy

1 The monarchy is important in governing the country.

In the UK a new government is elected every five years or so. Because the monarch is **head of state** for life, the monarchy can provide a stable background for the country during times of change.

At ceremonies like the **state opening of parliament**, the Queen is a powerful reminder of Britain's stable political history.

Although British monarchs do not take an active part in politics, they can have an important influence on the people who do. The Queen often has meetings with government **ministers**. They tell her what is happening, and she offers them advice.

The Queen has been on the throne for more than fifty years, and in that time there have been many changes of government. Ministers listen to her advice because they usually have far less experience of government than she does.

2 The monarchy is good value for money.

The Civil List is not a gift – it is a **salary**.

The Queen earns her money by carrying out all kinds of public duties, for example:

- advising her government

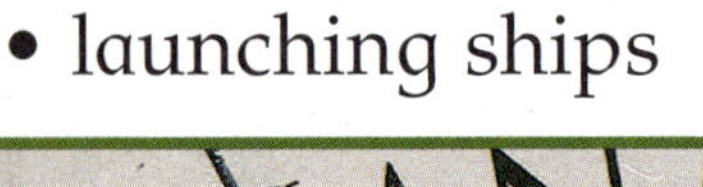

- launching ships

- going abroad on tours and representing the UK.

If the royal visits and ceremonies were less grand, they would be cheaper. But the splendour of displays like the changing of the guard at **Buckingham Palace** attracts a lot of tourists.

Tourism is an important industry in the UK.

Buckingham Palace
The Queen's residence in London

The Queen's image is everywhere:

- on postage stamps
- on coins and notes
- businesses carry her coat of arms, "By Royal Appointment"
- there is a Royal Mail
- there is a Royal Mint
- there is a Royal Air Force.

When the Queen lays her wreath on **Remembrance Sunday**, she acts on behalf of the British people in thanking those who died defending the country during World War I and World War II.

Because she is such an important part of the British national identity, the Queen can represent the UK in times of celebration or disaster.

When the Queen sends a message of sympathy to communities suffering because of floods or landslides, for example, people often feel she is speaking for the nation.

Remembrance Sunday

The Sunday nearest 11 November, when Britain remembers those who died during World War I and World War II

The Queen and her family do a lot of work for charities and social causes.

The Queen's daughter, Princesss Anne, is president of the Save the Children Fund, which works to help children all over the world.

Prince Charles set up the Prince's Trust, which offers advice, loans, grants and training to young people looking for work.

3 The monarchy is popular.

Even though the monarchy may seem out of date it is still popular. **Opinion polls** show that most people are in favour of keeping it. A lot of people feel genuine warmth and affection towards the royal family. Royal visits are treated with excitement.

Royals on Hols!

Prince Charles and his two sons, William and Harry, were spotted in sunny Scarborough this week.

Even people who aren't particularly fond of the royal family are fascinated by them. The smallest details of their lives are reported in the **media** both at home and abroad. People enjoy the glamour surrounding them.

QUEEN VISIT

Hundreds of proud members of the University of Nottingham turned out to meet the Queen on Monday. She travelled to Nottingham to open a new win of the education faculty, and everyone was delighted that she could attend.

PRINCE PICKS UNI!

Prince William chooses to study at St Andrews university when he returns from his year abroad.

SHE'S GOT THE LOT!

Royal fan has collected record amount of royal memorabilia. Her collection dates back to the nineteenth century and includes everything from royal mugs to silver jugs.

Why we should keep the monarchy but reform it

The monarchy does a good job and is an important part of national life in the UK. But if it is to stay, some changes will have to be made.

1 Changes to the traditions of the monarchy.

Some of its traditions, like making the sons of monarchs more important than the daughters, are no longer acceptable to most people.

Rules about how to behave in the presence of royalty are also unacceptable, like bowing and curtseying, and having to leave the room backwards so as not to turn your back on the monarch.

2 Changes in the way monarchs live.

Most modern monarchs lead a simpler lifestyle than the British Royal Family. Their households and expenses are smaller. Some people think the British monarch's lifestyle costs too much.

The Queen herself recognises the need for reform, and in 1993 she started paying **tax** on her income like everyone else.

Crown prince Haakon Norway seen shopping with fiancee, Mette Mar

The main objection people had to the civil list was that too many people were included in it. So in 1993 the number of people who received money in this way was reduced. Now only the Queen, her husband Prince Philip, and the Queen Mother are on the Civil List.

The Queen is also cutting down on the cost of transport. For example, in 1997 the Royal Yacht Britannia stopped serving the Queen and became a tourist attraction.

Before *(1954)*

After *(1998)*

Only the Royal Family used the yacht.

The public can go on a tour of the yacht.

3 Changes in the royal image.

Long ago, people thought kings and queens were different from everyone else, because they were specially chosen by God.

The Queen Mother and King George IV were looked up to by the British public.

More recently, people thought that even though they were not like gods, they were still different from everyone else because they were born into a position of leadership. They knew the rules and could show the people how to live by them.

But thanks to the modern media, everyone knows that even royal families have problems. Some of the Queen's children are divorced. Princess Diana was very unhappy. Other members of the royal family have had financial difficulties.

People used to look up to the monarch; they expected the monarch to show them the right way to live. Nowadays, people want the monarch to be more like themselves, to be someone they can identify with.

Summing up

The main arguments for getting rid of the monarchy are:

1. It hasn't got any real political power any more.
2. It costs too much money.
3. It is old-fashioned.

The main arguments for keeping it are:

1. It gives stability in a system of changing governments.
2. It is good value for money.
3. It is popular with the people.

The main arguments for keeping the monarchy but making some changes are:

1. It does a good job, but it needs to modernise in order to stay popular.
2. Changes in the traditions, lifestyle and image of the monarchy will make it more acceptable and effective in the modern world.

What do you think?

Does the UK still need the monarchy, or could an elected President do the Queen's job just as well? And if the UK wants to keep the monarchy, does it need to update some of its traditions and attitudes? Or would that take away some of its glamour, and make it less popular?